TABLE OF CONTENTS

INTRODUCTION

David Gilmour's journey to becoming one of the most iconic figures in rock history began with a spark of enthusiasm ignited in his early childhood. Growing up in Cambridge, England, Gilmour was surrounded by a nurturing environment that encouraged curiosity and exploration. His parents, Douglas and Sylvia Gilmour, were academically inclined individuals—his father a senior lecturer in zoology and his mother a teacher. Despite their intellectual pursuits, they fostered a home where creativity and self-expression flourished. It was within this supportive atmosphere that Gilmour's burgeoning passion for music found its first foothold.

In 1954, at the age of eight, Gilmour's interest in music was piqued when he purchased his first single, Bill Haley and His Comets' "Rock Around the Clock." The energetic rhythm and groundbreaking sound of rock 'n' roll captivated him, leaving an indelible mark on his young mind. A year later, this fascination deepened when he heard Elvis Presley's "Heartbreak Hotel." Presley's emotive voice and magnetic presence resonated with Gilmour, sparking an enduring appreciation for the transformative power of music. Around the same time, he discovered the Everly Brothers, whose harmonies and catchy melodies, particularly in "Bye Bye Love," ignited a growing interest in the guitar as a medium for self-expression.

Eager to turn his interest into action, Gilmour borrowed a guitar from a neighbor. This guitar, however, never found its way back to its original owner; it became the first in a long line of instruments that would shape his musical journey. With no formal training or lessons, Gilmour took it upon himself to learn the intricacies of the instrument. Armed with a book-and-record set by folk icon Pete Seeger, he began teaching himself the fundamentals of guitar playing. Seeger's instructional material, which combined practical guidance with auditory examples, laid the groundwork for Gilmour's early development as a guitarist.

This period of self-directed learning was pivotal. Gilmour's approach to the guitar was characterized by an innate curiosity and a willingness to experiment. He didn't merely replicate what he heard; instead, he absorbed the styles and techniques of his inspirations, gradually shaping them into his own. This method fostered a sense of individuality in his playing, a trait that would later become one of his most defining characteristics. By immersing himself in the music of artists like Presley and the Everly Brothers, he developed an intuitive understanding of melody and emotion, elements that would come to define his contributions to Pink Floyd and his solo work.

The Cambridge of Gilmour's youth was a city steeped in academia but also brimming with artistic and musical potential. Surrounded by open-minded thinkers and creators, Gilmour found a community that valued exploration and innovation. These formative years were not just about learning to play the guitar—they were about discovering the role that music could play in shaping one's identity and connecting with others.

As Gilmour honed his skills, his fascination with the guitar deepened. He began to see it not just as an instrument but as a voice—a means of communicating feelings and ideas that words could not adequately convey. This early realization would go on to inform his distinctive playing style, characterized by its lyrical phrasing and emotional depth.

Gilmour's path to greatness was never just about technical mastery. His early experiences underscore the importance of passion, curiosity, and resilience in the face of challenges. Unlike many aspiring musicians who rely on formal training, Gilmour's journey was largely self-driven. His ability to teach himself and adapt to different styles of music demonstrates not only his natural talent but also his unwavering dedication to his craft.

The support of his parents also played a crucial role. While they may not have been musicians themselves, their encouragement provided Gilmour with the confidence to pursue his passion wholeheartedly. In a world that often prioritizes conventional careers, the freedom to explore music as a legitimate path was a gift that Gilmour never took for granted. Their belief in his potential allowed him to thrive in an environment where creativity could flourish.

The foundation laid during Gilmour's formative years would eventually blossom into a career that redefined the possibilities of rock music. From his early days of strumming along to Pete Seeger's instructional records to crafting some of the most memorable solos in music history, Gilmour's journey is a testament to the power of perseverance and self-belief. These humble beginnings—a borrowed guitar, a few records, and an innate desire to create—set the stage for a lifetime of artistic achievement.

As we dive deeper into Gilmour's life and career, these early moments of discovery and inspiration remain at the heart of his story. They remind us that even the greatest legends start from modest beginnings, driven by a love for their craft and the determination to push boundaries. Gilmour's ability to channel his influences into something uniquely his own is what has made him one of the most revered figures in music history—a true visionary who found his voice and changed the sound of rock forever.

CHAPTER ONE

Early Days and Musical Awakening

David Jon Gilmour's journey began in Cambridge, England, a city steeped in intellectual history and artistic exploration. Born on March 6, 1946, into an academically inclined family, David grew up in an environment that nurtured curiosity and creativity. His father, Douglas Gilmour, was a senior lecturer in zoology at the University of Cambridge, while his mother, Sylvia, was a teacher and later became a film editor. This blend of academic rigor and creative insight would subtly influence David's approach to music and art throughout his life.

A Childhood in Cambridge

Cambridge in the 1940s and 50s was not just a center for academic excellence; it was also a place of cultural ferment. The city's scenic beauty, from the serene River Cam to the historic university buildings, provided an idyllic backdrop for David's formative years. His childhood was relatively ordinary but filled with opportunities for exploration. Cambridge's close-knit community and burgeoning arts scene exposed David to a world beyond textbooks and classrooms.

David's early years were marked by a natural curiosity and a love for learning. He excelled in school but often found himself drawn to artistic pursuits. As a boy, he developed an interest in drawing and painting, which reflected his keen eye for detail—a skill that would later translate into his meticulous approach to music production. While his academic surroundings encouraged intellectual growth, David found his true calling not in books but in the sound of music.

The Birth of a Musician

David's first encounter with music was through the radio, which introduced him to the rock-and-roll revolution sweeping through Britain. Artists like Elvis Presley, Chuck Berry, and Buddy Holly ignited his imagination, and their electrifying performances planted the seeds of a lifelong passion. At the age of 13, David received his first guitar, a cheap, used acoustic model that he cherished deeply. This humble instrument became his constant companion, sparking hours of self-taught practice.

Unlike many of his peers, David had no formal training. Instead, he relied on perseverance and an intuitive understanding of music. He spent hours playing along with records, meticulously imitating the sounds he admired. Early influences like Hank Marvin of The Shadows captivated him. Marvin's clean, melodic style, characterized by echo effects and precision, resonated deeply with David and left an indelible mark on his evolving technique.

The Cambridge Music Scene

During his teenage years, David began to immerse himself in Cambridge's burgeoning music scene. The city, while small, was home to a vibrant community of young musicians experimenting with new sounds. It was here that David first crossed paths with Syd Barrett, a charismatic and enigmatic figure who would later play a pivotal role in shaping David's destiny.

David and Syd met at the Cambridgeshire High School for Boys, where they bonded over a shared love of music and art.

Syd's free-spirited approach to creativity and David's disciplined yet experimental nature formed a unique camaraderie. Together, they spent countless hours listening to records, discussing art, and jamming on their guitars. Syd's influence on David was profound, inspiring him to view music not just as a technical craft but as a form of self-expression.

It was also during this time that David encountered Roger Waters, another Cambridge native who would become a key figure in Pink Floyd. While their early interactions were sporadic, they shared a mutual respect for each other's talents. The interconnectedness of the Cambridge music scene created a fertile ground for collaboration, laying the foundation for what would become one of rock's most iconic bands.

Joining Jokers Wild

David's first step into professional music came in 1962 when he joined Jokers Wild, a local band known for its polished performances of contemporary hits. The group quickly gained a reputation as one of Cambridge's premier acts, regularly performing at local venues and private events. For David, Jokers Wild was more than just a band; it was a proving ground. Here, he honed his stage presence, developed his technical skills, and began to experiment with different musical styles.

Jokers Wild recorded a limited-edition EP in 1965, which included covers of songs by The Drifters and The Miracles. While the record was not widely distributed, it marked David's first experience in a recording studio. The process of arranging and recording tracks fascinated him, igniting a passion for the technical aspects of music production that would later define his career.

During his time with Jokers Wild, David also began to explore the blues, a genre that deeply resonated with him. Inspired by legends like B.B. King, Lead Belly, and Muddy Waters, he incorporated blues-inspired bends and phrasing into his playing. This exploration added an emotional depth to his music, setting him apart from many of his contemporaries.

Life Beyond Music

While music was becoming an increasingly dominant force in David's life, he also pursued other interests. His parents encouraged him to focus on academics, and he briefly considered a career in the arts, given his talent for drawing and painting. However, his passion for the guitar proved too strong to ignore. Despite his parents' concerns about the uncertainty of a career in music, David remained determined to follow his dream.

In 1965, David embarked on a European adventure with friends, busking in cities like Paris and exploring the continent's cultural landscape. This period of travel broadened his horizons and deepened his appreciation for music as a universal language. It was also a time of personal growth, as David learned to navigate the challenges of life as an artist.

CHAPTER TWO

Joining Pink Floyd

The story of David Gilmour's entry into Pink Floyd in 1968 is a tale of transformation—for the band, for Gilmour himself, and for the future of rock music. It marked a pivotal shift in the band's trajectory as they transitioned from their Syd Barrett-led psychedelic beginnings to the broader, experimental soundscapes for which they would become legendary. This chapter explores the circumstances leading to Gilmour's invitation, his transition from supporting guitarist to lead, and how he established his role in Pink Floyd's evolving sound.

The Circumstances Leading to Gilmour's Invitation to Join Pink Floyd in 1968

By late 1967, Pink Floyd was both a band on the rise and a band in crisis. Their debut album, The Piper at the Gates of Dawn, had earned critical acclaim and commercial success, firmly positioning them as pioneers of the burgeoning British psychedelic scene. Songs like "Astronomy Domine" and

"Interstellar Overdrive" showcased the creative genius of Syd Barrett, the band's enigmatic frontman and principal songwriter.

However, Barrett's increasing dependence on LSD was taking a severe toll on his mental health. His unpredictable behavior and declining reliability became a significant problem during live performances and studio sessions. He often spaced out on stage, sometimes playing only a single chord or not playing at all. Offstage, he became withdrawn and detached, to the frustration and concern of his bandmates—Roger Waters, Nick Mason, and Richard Wright.

As Barrett's condition worsened, the remaining members of Pink Floyd recognized the need for a solution. They needed someone who could stabilize their live performances and potentially support Barrett in the studio. Enter David Gilmour, a guitarist whose reputation as a talented musician and longtime friend of Syd Barrett made him a natural choice.

Gilmour and Barrett had known each other since their school days in Cambridge. They had bonded over their shared love of music, often playing guitar together and exchanging ideas.

While Barrett's career with Pink Floyd was taking off in the mid-1960s, Gilmour had been pursuing his own musical path. After playing with Jokers Wild, Gilmour spent time busking in France and Spain, where he refined his craft and developed his melodic, emotive guitar style. By late 1967, Gilmour had returned to England, disillusioned with his European ventures but open to new opportunities.

In December 1967, Pink Floyd approached Gilmour with an invitation to join the band. The idea was to bring him in as a fifth member, initially as a second guitarist and vocalist to support Barrett. This arrangement was seen as a way to alleviate the pressure on Syd while maintaining the band's momentum. However, the reality quickly became apparent: Barrett was no longer capable of functioning in his role. By early 1968, Syd was effectively sidelined, and David Gilmour became Pink Floyd's new lead guitarist.

Transitioning from Supporting Syd Barrett to Becoming the Lead Guitarist

The transition from being a supporting guitarist to taking on the role of Pink Floyd's lead guitarist was not an easy one for

Gilmour. The band was still reeling from the emotional and creative loss of Syd Barrett, whose unique vision had defined their early sound. Gilmour faced the dual challenge of filling Syd's shoes while carving out his own identity within the group.

Initially, Gilmour's role was to replicate Barrett's parts during live performances. This was no small task, as Syd's unconventional playing style and use of effects pedals were central to the band's sound. Gilmour approached this responsibility with respect for Barrett's legacy, carefully studying his techniques and adding his own touches to the performances. Songs like "See Emily Play" and "Arnold Layne" remained staples of their setlists, and Gilmour's ability to emulate Barrett's style helped the band maintain their connection to their early work.

As Pink Floyd moved forward, it became clear that Gilmour's contributions would extend far beyond simply replicating Syd's work. His technical proficiency and melodic sensibilities brought a new dimension to the band's music. While Barrett's playing had been raw and instinctive, Gilmour's approach was more refined and emotive, with a focus on tone and phrasing.

This shift in style marked the beginning of Pink Floyd's evolution from psychedelic rock to the more atmospheric and expansive soundscapes that would define their later work.

Gilmour's transition was solidified during the recording of A Saucerful of Secrets (1968), the band's second album and the first to feature him. While much of the material had been developed before his arrival, Gilmour's contributions were crucial. He played on tracks like "Let There Be More Light" and "Set the Controls for the Heart of the Sun," infusing them with his distinctive guitar work. On the album's title track, his use of slide guitar and effects hinted at the sonic experimentation that would become a hallmark of Pink Floyd's music.

Establishing His Role in the Band's Evolving Sound

As Gilmour became more integrated into Pink Floyd, he began to play a central role in shaping their evolving sound. His guitar playing became a defining element of the band's identity, characterized by its emotional depth, melodic clarity, and innovative use of technology. Gilmour was not merely a replacement for Syd Barrett; he was a transformative force who helped Pink Floyd explore new musical territories.

One of Gilmour's key contributions was his ability to balance technical skill with emotional resonance. Unlike many of his contemporaries, who focused on speed and complexity, Gilmour prioritized tone, phrasing, and atmosphere. His solos were not just showcases of technical prowess; they were integral to the storytelling of the music. This approach would later culminate in iconic solos like those in "Comfortably Numb" and "Shine On You Crazy Diamond."

Gilmour's influence extended beyond his guitar playing. He also became a significant vocal presence in the band, often sharing lead vocal duties with Roger Waters and Richard Wright. His rich, smooth voice provided a counterpoint to Waters' more aggressive style, adding depth and variety to the band's sound.

As Pink Floyd moved into the post-Barrett era, they began to experiment with longer compositions and conceptual themes. Gilmour's contributions were instrumental in this process, as his ability to create evocative soundscapes complemented the band's increasingly ambitious vision. Tracks like "Careful with That Axe, Eugene" and "Echoes" showcased his mastery of dynamics, texture, and emotion.

CHAPTER THREE

A Sonic Architect

David Gilmour's role in Pink Floyd was more than that of a guitarist; he became a sonic architect, helping to construct the band's signature sound that would captivate audiences and define progressive rock. Through his innovative guitar techniques, emotive solos, and an ear for experimentation, Gilmour shaped not only Pink Floyd's musical identity but also the broader landscape of rock music. This chapter explores Gilmour's contributions to the band's iconic sound, his development as a guitarist, and the creative process behind Meddle (1971), the album that laid the groundwork for The Dark Side of the Moon (1973).

Gilmour's Contribution to Pink Floyd's Iconic Sound

When Gilmour joined Pink Floyd in 1968, the band was at a crossroads. Syd Barrett's departure had left a creative vacuum, and the remaining members were searching for a new direction. Gilmour's arrival not only stabilized the band but also opened up new musical possibilities. His ability to combine technical precision with emotional depth became a cornerstone of Pink Floyd's sound, helping the band transition from their psychedelic roots to more sophisticated, conceptual music.

At the heart of Gilmour's contribution was his ability to create music that resonated emotionally. Unlike many guitarists of his era, who focused on speed and technical showmanship, Gilmour emphasized melody, tone, and atmosphere. His solos often felt like narratives within the larger story of a song, drawing listeners into the emotional core of the music. This approach was evident in early tracks like "Echoes," where his guitar lines acted as both a guiding melody and a textural element, weaving seamlessly with the rest of the arrangement.

Gilmour's understanding of dynamics also played a crucial role in Pink Floyd's sound. He was a master of building tension and releasing it in ways that felt both dramatic and natural. Whether it was the subtle build-up in "Fearless" or the explosive climax of "Echoes," Gilmour's ability to manipulate sound and structure gave Pink Floyd's music a sense of grandeur and depth.

Development of Gilmour's Guitar Techniques and Distinctive Tone

David Gilmour's guitar playing is instantly recognizable, defined by its emotive phrasing, soaring melodies, and meticulous attention to tone. Developing this signature style was a gradual process, influenced by a combination of early inspirations, experimentation, and a deep commitment to the craft.

One of the defining aspects of Gilmour's playing is his use of bends and vibrato. Inspired by blues legends like B.B. King and Albert King, Gilmour adopted these techniques to give his playing a vocal-like quality. Each note was carefully chosen and imbued with feeling, often conveying more emotion than lyrics could. This approach made Gilmour's solos memorable and deeply affecting.

Another key element of Gilmour's sound was his innovative use of effects pedals and studio technology. During the recording of Meddle, he began experimenting extensively with tools like the Binson Echorec, a multi-tap delay unit that allowed him to create the ethereal, echoing sounds heard on tracks like "One of These Days." The Echorec became a staple of Gilmour's rig, enabling him to craft the atmospheric textures that would define much of Pink Floyd's music in the 1970s.

Gilmour also developed a distinctive approach to slide guitar, using it not just for bluesy licks but as a tool for creating ambient soundscapes. On "Echoes," for instance, his slide work added a haunting, otherworldly quality that became a central part of the track's mood. His use of alternate tunings, layering techniques, and carefully sculpted feedback further expanded his sonic palette, allowing him to push the boundaries of what the guitar could do.

Tone was another area where Gilmour excelled. He spent hours refining his sound, often combining different amps, pickups, and effects to achieve the perfect balance of warmth, clarity, and sustain. His legendary 1969 Fender Stratocaster, known as the "Black Strat," became his main instrument and was instrumental in shaping his tone. Paired with amps like the Hiwatt Custom 100 and effects like the Uni-Vibe and Fuzz

Face, the Black Strat produced the rich, expressive sound that defined Gilmour's playing.

The Making of Meddle and Sonic Experimentation

The creation of Meddle marked a turning point for Pink Floyd and for David Gilmour as a guitarist and composer. Released in 1971, the album was the band's most ambitious work to date, showcasing their growing confidence in blending experimental techniques with accessible melodies. For Gilmour, Meddle was an opportunity to fully explore his role as a sonic architect, shaping the album's sound through both his playing and his approach to production.

Crafting "Echoes"

The centerpiece of Meddle was "Echoes," a 23-minute epic that occupied the entire second side of the album. Gilmour's contributions to the track were monumental, both in terms of his guitar work and his role in the composition process. The iconic opening, created by Gilmour running a single note through a Leslie speaker cabinet, set the tone for the track's underwater, dreamlike atmosphere.

Throughout "Echoes," Gilmour's guitar served as a unifying thread, weaving together the song's disparate sections. His slide guitar, delay effects, and layered harmonics created a sense of vastness and exploration, perfectly complementing the track's themes of connection and discovery. The climactic solo, with its soaring bends and sustained notes, became one of Gilmour's most iconic performances, embodying the emotional power of his playing.

Exploration on "One of These Days"

"One of These Days," the album's opening track, was another showcase of Gilmour's sonic experimentation. Built around a pulsating bass line played by both Gilmour and Roger Waters, the track featured Gilmour's searing slide guitar and heavy use of the Binson Echorec. The result was a hypnotic, otherworldly sound that captured the band's ability to fuse raw energy with atmospheric depth.

Subtlety in "Fearless"

On "Fearless," Gilmour demonstrated a more restrained side of his playing. The track, built around an open G tuning, featured a gently arpeggiated riff that underscored the song's introspective lyrics. Gilmour's ability to balance simplicity with emotional resonance was on full display, proving that his genius lay not just in grand solos but also in the quiet moments.

Studio Innovation

The recording sessions for Meddle were characterized by a spirit of experimentation. Gilmour and the band spent hours in the studio, testing new ideas and pushing the limits of the available technology. They used tape loops, custom-built equipment, and unconventional recording techniques to achieve their desired sounds. Gilmour's technical knowledge and willingness to experiment played a key role in this process, earning him a reputation as both a musician and a producer.

Laying the Groundwork for The Dark Side of the Moon

Meddle was a critical and creative stepping stone for Pink Floyd, and David Gilmour's contributions were central to its success. The album's blend of structured compositions and experimental textures laid the groundwork for The Dark Side of the Moon, the band's breakthrough masterpiece. Gilmour's ability to create evocative soundscapes and emotionally charged solos became even more pronounced on Dark Side, cementing his status as one of rock's most innovative guitarists.

The lessons learned during the making of Meddle—from the use of effects to the integration of conceptual themes—would inform the band's approach moving forward. Gilmour's role as a sonic architect was firmly established, and his influence would continue to shape Pink Floyd's music for decades to come.

CHAPTER FOUR

The Dark Side of the Moon and Global SUCCESS

The release of The Dark Side of the Moon in 1973 was a seismic moment in the history of music. The album elevated Pink Floyd from an experimental, progressive rock band to global superstars, establishing them as one of the most influential groups of all time. Central to this achievement was David Gilmour, whose contributions as a guitarist, vocalist, and sonic visionary played a pivotal role in shaping the album's timeless appeal. This chapter explores Gilmour's creative role in the making of The Dark Side of the Moon, the album's unprecedented global impact, and the shifting dynamics within Pink Floyd during their meteoric rise to fame.

Gilmour's Pivotal Role in Shaping The Dark Side of the Moon (1973)

The Dark Side of the Moon was a product of meticulous planning, collaborative effort, and artistic ambition. Conceived as a conceptual album that explored universal themes such as time, mortality, mental illness, and greed, the record demanded a unified sound that was both accessible and innovative. David Gilmour was instrumental in achieving this balance, contributing not only his distinctive guitar work but also his vocal talents, production skills, and creative ideas.

Guitar Work and Sound Design

Gilmour's guitar playing on The Dark Side of the Moon is among the most celebrated in rock history. His solos and textures added emotional depth and cinematic grandeur to the album's songs, creating moments of intense beauty and introspection.

One of the standout tracks, "Time," showcases Gilmour's ability to blend technical prowess with emotional resonance. The song's iconic guitar solo, featuring sustained notes and expressive bends, is a masterclass in musical storytelling. Gilmour's deliberate phrasing and impeccable tone capture the song's meditation on the fleeting nature of life, making it one of the album's most memorable moments.

On "Money," Gilmour's blues-infused solo cuts through the song's rhythmic complexity, adding an edge to its critique of materialism. His use of pentatonic scales and rhythmic syncopation reflects his roots in blues and rock while demonstrating his innovative approach to soloing within an unconventional time signature (7/4).

Gilmour's contributions extended beyond solos to the atmospheric layers that defined the album's sound. Using tools like the Binson Echorec, Uni-Vibe, and carefully crafted reverb settings, he created lush, enveloping soundscapes. These textures, heard in tracks like "Breathe (In the Air)" and "Us and Them," gave the album its dreamlike quality, inviting listeners into its introspective world.

Vocal Contributions

Gilmour's voice was as integral to The Dark Side of the Moon as his guitar. His smooth, melodic delivery provided a counterpoint to Roger Waters' more biting vocal style, creating a dynamic interplay that enriched the album's storytelling.

Gilmour's lead vocals on tracks like "Breathe (In the Air)" and "Time" capture the album's reflective tone. His ability to convey emotion without overstatement became a hallmark of Pink Floyd's music, drawing listeners into the philosophical themes explored in the lyrics.

Songwriting and Collaboration

While The Dark Side of the Moon is often associated with Roger Waters' conceptual vision and lyrics, the music itself was a product of collaborative effort. Gilmour's role in shaping the melodies and arrangements was vital to the album's success. His contributions to tracks like "Breathe (In the Air)," "Time," and "Any Colour You Like" reflect his melodic sensibilities and his knack for creating songs that are both complex and accessible.

The band's approach to crafting the album was highly experimental. They used the studio as an instrument, incorporating tape loops, sound effects, and innovative recording techniques. Gilmour's technical expertise and willingness to push boundaries made him a key player in these experiments. His input helped ensure that the album's sonic innovations served its thematic narrative, rather than overshadowing it.

Global Impact and Critical Acclaim of the Album

The release of The Dark Side of the Moon on March 1, 1973, was met with immediate acclaim. Critics praised its seamless integration of music and theme, its groundbreaking production, and its emotional resonance. The album's universal appeal quickly translated into commercial success, catapulting Pink Floyd to international stardom.

The Dark Side of the Moon became a cultural phenomenon, resonating with audiences across generations and geographies. Its exploration of existential themes struck a chord with listeners navigating the social and political upheavals of the 1970s. Tracks like "Us and Them" and "Brain Damage" addressed issues of war, division, and mental health with a depth and sensitivity rarely seen in popular music.

Commercially, the album was an unprecedented success. It topped charts worldwide, including a historic run of 741 weeks on the Billboard 200 chart in the United States—a record unmatched by any other album. By the end of the 20th century, The Dark Side of the Moon had achieved remarkable commercial success, with sales surpassing 45 million copies worldwide, cementing its status as one of the highest-selling albums in history.

The album's success also cemented Pink Floyd's reputation as pioneers of album-oriented rock. Unlike many of their contemporaries, who focused on singles, Pink Floyd created an immersive listening experience designed to be enjoyed in its entirety. Gilmour's contributions to this holistic approach—his ability to balance technical innovation with emotional impact—were critical to its success.

The Dynamics Within the Band During Their Rise to Fame

While The Dark Side of the Moon brought Pink Floyd unparalleled success, it also marked the beginning of shifting dynamics within the band. As the group's profile rose, so did the tensions among its members, particularly between Gilmour and Roger Waters.

Gilmour, whose contributions were often understated, began to feel overshadowed by Waters' growing dominance in the band's creative direction. While Waters was the primary lyricist and conceptual architect, Gilmour's role in crafting the music and sound was equally vital. The disparity in recognition would later become a point of contention, as the band's creative process became increasingly contentious in subsequent years.

Despite these underlying tensions, the making of The Dark Side of the Moon was a period of relative harmony for Pink Floyd. The band's shared commitment to excellence and innovation fostered a collaborative spirit that allowed each member to shine. For Gilmour, this era represented the height of his creative synergy with the band—a time when his vision as a guitarist and sonic architect was fully realized.

The demands of fame, however, took their toll. The global success of The Dark Side of the Moon thrust Pink Floyd into the limelight, with relentless touring and media attention straining their personal and professional relationships. Gilmour, known for his reserved and introspective nature, often struggled with the pressures of fame. Yet he remained committed to the music, channeling his experiences into his playing and helping Pink Floyd navigate their newfound status as rock icons.

CHAPTER FIVE

The Wall of Emotion

The release of The Wall in 1979 marked one of Pink Floyd's most ambitious projects and a turning point in the band's history. It was a sprawling rock opera, largely conceived by Roger Waters, that delved into themes of alienation, mental anguish, and personal isolation. Amidst the album's grandeur and dark introspection, David Gilmour's contributions stood out as both artistic highlights and essential components of the project's success. However, the making of The Wall was also fraught with tension, particularly between Gilmour and Waters, as creative differences and personal conflicts reached new heights. This chapter examines Gilmour's pivotal role in shaping the music of The Wall, the tensions that defined its creation, and the creative highs and interpersonal struggles that characterized Pink Floyd's later years.

Gilmour's Contributions to The Wall (1979)

While The Wall is often regarded as Roger Waters' magnum opus, David Gilmour's musical contributions were indispensable. His distinctive guitar work, melodic sensibilities, and vocal performances brought emotional depth and sonic power to the album, elevating it beyond a mere conceptual narrative.

"Comfortably Numb"

No discussion of Gilmour's role in The Wall would be complete without addressing "Comfortably Numb," one of the most iconic songs in Pink Floyd's catalog. The track is a collaboration between Waters and Gilmour, combining Waters' introspective lyrics with Gilmour's soaring musical composition. Gilmour's haunting vocal performance on the verses, paired with Waters' more impassioned delivery in the choruses, creates a dynamic contrast that mirrors the song's themes of detachment and internal conflict.

The song's two guitar solos are often cited as among the greatest in rock history. Gilmour's masterful use of phrasing, bends, and sustain imbues the solos with an almost operatic quality, perfectly conveying the protagonist's emotional numbness. The final solo, in particular, is a tour de force, building to a cathartic crescendo that encapsulates the despair and transcendence at the heart of the song.

Gilmour's perfectionism during the recording process was evident in his painstaking approach to crafting the solos. He experimented with different guitar setups, effects, and amplifiers to achieve the warm, searing tone that defines the track. The result is a performance that remains a benchmark for expressive guitar playing.

Other Key Contributions

Gilmour's influence extends beyond "Comfortably Numb" to several other tracks on The Wall. On "Run Like Hell," Gilmour co-wrote the music with Waters, crafting the driving rhythm and ominous guitar riffs that underpin the song's sense of paranoia. His use of echo and delay effects adds a menacing, futuristic quality to the track, reinforcing its themes of fear and oppression.

Gilmour's vocals shine on "Young Lust," a hard-edged rocker that provides a moment of levity amidst the album's heavier themes. His bluesy delivery and gritty guitar work bring an energy and immediacy to the track, contrasting with the introspective tone of much of the album.

Throughout The Wall, Gilmour's guitar serves as both a narrative device and an emotional anchor. Whether providing delicate textures on tracks like "Goodbye Blue Sky" or searing leads on "Another Brick in the Wall, Part II," his playing enhances the album's storytelling and emotional impact.

Exploring the Tensions Between Gilmour and Roger Waters

The making of The Wall was marked by intense creative tensions between David Gilmour and Roger Waters. By the late 1970s, Waters had assumed a dominant role within Pink Floyd, driving the band's conceptual direction and asserting greater control over its output. This shift in dynamics created friction, as Gilmour and the other members of the band often felt sidelined in the creative process.

Gilmour's collaborative nature clashed with Waters' increasingly authoritarian approach. While Waters valued Gilmour's musical contributions, he often resisted input that deviated from his own vision. Gilmour, in turn, grew frustrated with what he perceived as Waters' reluctance to acknowledge the importance of the band's collective effort.

One of the most contentious issues during the production of The Wall was the delegation of credit. Gilmour's significant contributions, particularly on tracks like "Comfortably Numb" and "Run Like Hell," were occasionally overshadowed by the narrative of Waters as the album's sole architect. This dynamic led to growing resentment, as Gilmour felt his role in shaping the band's sound and success was not fully recognized.

The tensions extended beyond creative disagreements to interpersonal conflicts. The pressures of recording such an ambitious album, coupled with the demands of fame and the band's fractured relationships, created a toxic atmosphere. Despite these challenges, Gilmour maintained his professionalism, focusing on delivering performances that would serve the music and the project as a whole.

The Creative Highs and Interpersonal Struggles of Pink Floyd's Later Years

The completion of The Wall was both a triumph and a turning point for Pink Floyd. The album's success was staggering, becoming one of the best-selling records of all time and spawning a critically acclaimed stage show and a feature film. For Gilmour, however, the experience was bittersweet.

The creative highs of The Wall were tempered by the growing realization that Pink Floyd's collaborative spirit was eroding. The recording sessions were often fragmented, with Gilmour and Waters working separately or with limited interaction. Keyboardist Richard Wright was even forced out of the band during the sessions, further highlighting the breakdown in relationships.

Gilmour's role during this period was one of balance—he sought to contribute meaningfully to the music while navigating the personal and professional challenges within the band. His ability to focus on the artistic integrity of the project, even amidst conflict, was a testament to his dedication and resilience.

The interpersonal struggles came to a head during the tour for The Wall, which was as logistically complex as it was artistically ambitious. The tension between Gilmour and Waters often spilled over into rehearsals and performances, straining their already fragile partnership. Despite these challenges, Gilmour's live performances, particularly on tracks like "Comfortably Numb," became defining moments of the shows, earning widespread acclaim.

CHAPTER SIX

Going Solo

By the late 1970s, David Gilmour was well-established as one of the defining musicians of his generation, but his creative journey was far from confined to Pink Floyd. The release of his self-titled debut solo album in 1978 marked the beginning of Gilmour's exploration as an independent artist, allowing him to step out of the shadow of the band and showcase his personal musical identity. This chapter delves into the creation of David Gilmour, his early forays into solo work, and how he balanced his burgeoning solo career with his commitments to Pink Floyd.

The Release of David Gilmour (1978)

The seeds of David Gilmour's solo career were planted during a turbulent period in Pink Floyd's history. Following the monumental success of Wish You Were Here (1975), the band had struggled with internal tensions and creative differences. The recording of Animals (1977) had further highlighted these divides, with Roger Waters assuming a dominant role in the band's creative direction. For Gilmour, these dynamics often left him with limited space to express his own musical ideas.

Motivated by a desire for creative freedom, Gilmour began work on his first solo album in 1978. The project was a deeply personal endeavor, with Gilmour serving as the primary writer, performer, and producer. Recorded at Super Bear Studios in the south of France, David Gilmour featured a stripped-down approach that contrasted with the grandiosity of Pink Floyd's work.

Musical Style and Themes

The album highlighted Gilmour's strengths as a guitarist and vocalist, showcasing his ability to craft melodic, emotionally resonant music. Tracks like "There's No Way Out of Here" and "Cry from the Street" blended introspective lyrics with atmospheric guitar work, reflecting Gilmour's distinctive style. "There's No Way Out of Here," in particular, became a standout track, with its haunting melody and melancholic tone earning critical acclaim and radio play.

Instrumentally, the album emphasized Gilmour's mastery of the guitar. From the soaring solos to the intricate fingerpicking, his playing demonstrated a range and depth that further cemented his reputation as one of rock's premier guitarists. The album's production, though more modest than Pink Floyd's elaborate soundscapes, allowed Gilmour's artistry to shine in a more intimate setting.

Collaborations and Contributions

While David Gilmour was largely a solo effort, it also featured contributions from talented collaborators. Rick Wills (bass) and Willie Wilson (drums), both of whom had worked with Gilmour in the past, provided a solid rhythmic foundation for the album. The trio's chemistry was evident in the album's cohesive sound, with each musician complementing Gilmour's vision.

Balancing Solo Work with Pink Floyd Commitments

Gilmour's decision to embark on a solo project did not signal a departure from Pink Floyd. Rather, it was an opportunity for him to explore his own musical identity while maintaining his role within the band. This balance was not without its challenges, as the pressures of sustaining one of the world's most successful rock groups often demanded Gilmour's full attention.

The Impact on Pink Floyd

The release of David Gilmour came at a pivotal moment for Pink Floyd. The band was gearing up for the creation of The Wall (1979), a project that would ultimately be defined by Roger Waters' creative vision. For Gilmour, his solo work provided a necessary outlet, allowing him to channel his musical ideas independently of the band's evolving dynamic.

While Gilmour's solo pursuits occasionally created friction within Pink Floyd, they also enriched his contributions to the band. His experiences as a solo artist helped him refine his songwriting and production skills, which would prove invaluable during the making of The Wall. Tracks like "Comfortably Numb" and "Run Like Hell" bore the hallmarks of Gilmour's solo explorations, blending his melodic sensibilities with the band's conceptual ambition.

Early Experiments with Songwriting and Collaboration

Gilmour's first solo album marked the beginning of his journey as an independent songwriter and collaborator. Unlike the often hierarchical structure of Pink Floyd, his solo work allowed him to experiment freely, drawing inspiration from a variety of genres and influences.

Exploration of Personal Themes

The lyrics on David Gilmour reflected a more personal and introspective perspective than much of Pink Floyd's work. While the band often tackled grand, universal themes, Gilmour's solo material delved into more intimate territory, exploring feelings of isolation, longing, and self-discovery. This thematic shift underscored Gilmour's desire to express his individual voice as an artist.

Building Collaborative Networks

In addition to his work with Rick Wills and Willie Wilson, Gilmour began to establish relationships with other musicians and producers during this period. These collaborations would play a significant role in shaping his subsequent solo projects, as Gilmour sought to expand his musical horizons and experiment with different styles.

One notable example was his collaboration with Roy Harper, a folk-rock artist with whom Gilmour had developed a close friendship. Gilmour had previously contributed guitar work to Harper's 1975 album HQ, and the two musicians shared a mutual respect for each other's talents. This partnership highlighted Gilmour's willingness to step outside the confines of Pink Floyd's progressive rock framework and engage with a broader musical community.

Reception and Legacy of David Gilmour

Upon its release, David Gilmour received a warm but measured response from critics and fans. While some praised its stripped-down aesthetic and focus on Gilmour's guitar work, others viewed it as a more modest offering compared to Pink Floyd's ambitious catalog. Commercially, the album performed respectably, reaching the top 30 on the UK charts and the top 50 in the US.

Over time, David Gilmour has been recognized as an important milestone in Gilmour's career. The album not only showcased his abilities as a solo artist but also laid the groundwork for his later solo projects, including About Face (1984), On an Island (2006), and Rattle That Lock (2015). For Gilmour, the experience of creating his debut solo album was a formative one, providing him with the confidence and skills to navigate the challenges of both his solo career and his continued role within Pink Floyd.

CHAPTER SEVEN

A New Era: Post-Waters Pink Floyd

The dissolution of Pink Floyd's core creative partnership in the mid-1980s, marked by Roger Waters' departure and the subsequent legal battles over the band's name, marked the beginning of an entirely new chapter for David Gilmour and Pink Floyd. The period following Waters' exit was fraught with challenges, from public scrutiny to internal doubts. Yet, under Gilmour's leadership, Pink Floyd not only survived but thrived. This chapter delves into the complexities surrounding the breakup of Pink Floyd's classic lineup, the rise of A Momentary Lapse of Reason (1987), and the difficulties Gilmour faced as he carried the band's legacy into a new era.

The Breakup with Roger Waters and Legal Battles Over the Band's Name

The origins of Pink Floyd's fracture can be traced back to the making of The Wall (1979). While the album's success solidified the band's place in rock history, it also highlighted growing tensions between Roger Waters and the rest of the group. Waters had increasingly assumed creative and conceptual control, to the point where his demands alienated both Gilmour and drummer Nick Mason. The result was a volatile working environment that would come to a head after The Wall tour ended.

By the early 1980s, Waters had taken full command of Pink Floyd's direction, pushing aside Gilmour's contributions both musically and creatively. In 1985, Roger Waters shocked the world by declaring that Pink Floyd was "a spent force" and that the band was essentially over. With Waters' departure, Gilmour and Mason were left to pick up the pieces of a broken band, but the legal battles that followed would be nothing short of grueling.

Legal Struggles and Waters' Departure

Waters believed that his departure gave him control over the name "Pink Floyd" and the rights to the band's legacy. He argued that without him, the band could not continue under its iconic name. This led to a legal dispute between Waters and the remaining members of Pink Floyd. The legal wrangling over the use of the band's name and assets threatened to derail Gilmour and Mason's efforts to continue the band's journey.

Gilmour, however, felt that Pink Floyd was more than just one individual's vision—it was a collective creative effort that had always been shaped by the contributions of multiple members. Gilmour and Mason fought tirelessly to retain the rights to Pink Floyd's name, and after a protracted legal battle, they emerged victorious, allowing them to continue making music as Pink Floyd.

Despite the victory, the relationship between Gilmour and Waters became irreparably strained, and the two would not speak for years after the lawsuit. The deep personal and creative rift would eventually find its way into the public eye, with Waters often vocal in his criticism of Gilmour's leadership of the band.

The Rebirth of Pink Floyd: A Momentary Lapse of Reason (1987)

With the legal disputes settled, Pink Floyd faced the daunting task of rebuilding itself without its primary conceptual mastermind. Gilmour, however, was determined to continue the band, undeterred by the personal and professional challenges ahead. His vision was to breathe new life into Pink Floyd while remaining true to the legacy they had created together.

The result was A Momentary Lapse of Reason, released in 1987. It marked a significant turning point for the band, as Gilmour took on the role of both lead guitarist and primary creative force. While the album was unmistakably Pink Floyd in terms of its lush production and sound, it also reflected Gilmour's individual style as a songwriter and musician.

Musical Direction and Creative Freedom

A Momentary Lapse of Reason showcased a clear departure from the band's previous, more collaborative approach. Gilmour's influence over the album's direction was more pronounced than it had ever been. The album incorporated some of Pink Floyd's signature sonic qualities—sweeping synthesizers, atmospheric soundscapes, and Gilmour's emotive guitar work—while also experimenting with new elements like the use of sampled sounds and modern production techniques.

The lyrical themes of the album reflected a sense of searching and introspection. Tracks like "Learning to Fly" and "On the Turning Away" focused on personal freedom, renewal, and introspection, addressing both universal and intimate experiences. While these themes resonated with fans, the album also signaled a shift in Pink Floyd's sound, with the focus now more on Gilmour's individual perspective rather than the conceptual, narrative-driven approach that had dominated previous works.

The album's creation was a collaborative effort with new contributors like producer Bob Ezrin, who had worked with Pink Floyd on The Wall, and new session musicians. The album also featured contributions from drummer Nick Mason, but it was clear that Pink Floyd was now functioning as a more loose collective than the tight-knit unit of old.

Critical Reception and Success

A Momentary Lapse of Reason was met with mixed reviews. While some praised the album's atmospheric quality and Gilmour's guitar work, others criticized it for lacking the depth and cohesion of Pink Floyd's earlier albums, particularly those created under the influence of Waters. Many fans were disappointed by the absence of the band's former conceptual focus, but A Momentary Lapse of Reason was nevertheless a commercial success. The album reached the top of the charts in both the UK and the US, securing Pink Floyd's place in the post-Waters era.

The accompanying tour, which was one of the most elaborate and successful in Pink Floyd's history, helped re-establish the band as one of the premier live acts in rock music. The tour featured an impressive light show, pyrotechnics, and a vast array of multimedia effects, reinforcing Pink Floyd's reputation for pushing the boundaries of live performance.

Challenges of Carrying the Pink Floyd Legacy Forward

For Gilmour, the challenge of carrying Pink Floyd's legacy forward was not only artistic but personal. While A Momentary Lapse of Reason had successfully introduced a new phase of Pink Floyd's sound, Gilmour faced continued pressure to prove that the band could survive without Waters. As the leader of a band that had once been a defining force of progressive rock, Gilmour was constantly under scrutiny—by critics, by fans, and, most of all, by Waters himself.

The Weight of Expectations

There was an inherent tension in the air as Pink Floyd moved forward. Gilmour, while undoubtedly the band's creative and technical leader, was constantly compared to Waters. Fans who had grown up with the conceptually rich albums of the 1970s were often hesitant to embrace the more straightforward sound that emerged on A Momentary Lapse of Reason. There were some, especially within the progressive rock community, who felt that Pink Floyd had lost its soul after Waters' departure.

Yet Gilmour was unwavering in his commitment to keeping Pink Floyd alive. He was resolute in the belief that the band was more than just a collaboration of ideas between him and Waters—it was an institution, one that had created a lasting musical legacy. Gilmour's approach to the band's future was clear: he wanted to retain the band's musical integrity while giving it a new direction, one that allowed him to express his own ideas.

A key element of Gilmour's leadership was the careful balance he struck between honoring the band's past and charting a new course. Pink Floyd's sound on A Momentary Lapse of Reason was rooted in their previous work, with clear echoes of albums like Wish You Were Here (1975) and Animals (1977). Yet, Gilmour's songwriting on this album was more introspective and personal, as he sought to capture the emotional resonance of Pink Floyd's sound without relying on the grand conceptual themes that had characterized the band's earlier albums.

By introducing new musicians and collaborators, Gilmour revitalized Pink Floyd's sound, but he also faced the challenge of keeping the band's identity intact. The tension between innovation and legacy was palpable throughout the recording process, and it was clear that, for Gilmour, maintaining Pink Floyd's legacy was as important as shaping its future.

CHAPTER EIGHT

The Division Bell and the Last Floyd Era

By the early 1990s, Pink Floyd had firmly re-established themselves as one of the most influential bands in rock history. Despite their resurgence after the departure of Roger Waters in the 1980s, the band faced immense personal and professional challenges in maintaining their iconic legacy. The Division Bell (1994), Pink Floyd's fourteenth studio album, marked the final chapter in the band's storied career. This album was not only a culmination of their post-Waters journey but also a reflection of the band's struggles with communication, both personally and artistically. In this chapter, we explore the making of The Division Bell, its themes of communication and reconciliation, and Pink Floyd's enduring legacy as they entered their final era together.

The Making of The Division Bell (1994)

The creation of The Division Bell came at a time when Pink Floyd had achieved a somewhat fragile peace. After the success of A Momentary Lapse of Reason (1987), which had brought the band back into the limelight, the members of Pink Floyd were once again working together, though the band dynamic was still complicated. Gilmour and Mason had remained constant in the band, but the absence of Roger Waters, the creative force behind much of Pink Floyd's most famous work, had left a void. The internal tensions that had caused the band's initial breakup in the 1980s were far from resolved, but they had learned to coexist, at least in the professional sense.

The production of The Division Bell took place from 1993 to 1994, primarily at the band's own studios, Britannia Row, and Astoria, Gilmour's houseboat studio on the River Thames. Gilmour took on the primary role of creative leader, guiding the album's direction while also collaborating closely with keyboardist Richard Wright, who had become an integral part of the band's sound once again after being largely sidelined during the Waters era. The recording process was far less contentious than the sessions for The Wall or A Momentary Lapse of Reason. However, the album was still marked by subtle undercurrents of tension, as Gilmour and Mason often found themselves dealing with the remnants of past conflicts while attempting to forge something new.

The album was characterized by its lush, atmospheric sound, a blend of Pink Floyd's signature sonic landscape with more modern production techniques. The material was more polished and refined than previous efforts, showcasing the band's ability to craft immersive soundscapes. While it contained elements that were reminiscent of The Wall and A Momentary Lapse of Reason, The Division Bell also offered something fresh, a sense of emotional depth that had been somewhat absent from their earlier post-Waters work.

Collaborators and Contributions

The album featured contributions from several talented musicians. Among the most notable was guitarist Tim Renwick, who had been a session musician on earlier albums and now played a larger role in the band's live performances. The saxophone playing of Dick Parry, who had famously contributed to Dark Side of the Moon (1973), also returned to add another layer of texture to the album's sound.

However, The Division Bell was also marked by the absence of Roger Waters, who, despite not being involved in the recording, continued to be a significant presence in the public perception of Pink Floyd. His absence was a complicated matter for the band—though his departure had cleared the way for Gilmour to assume creative control, Waters' shadow loomed large over the band, and his influence could still be felt in the lyrical and thematic structures of The Division Bell.

Themes of Communication and Reconciliation

At its core, The Division Bell is an album about communication—both its failures and its potential for reconciliation. Gilmour, in particular, used the album as an opportunity to address the fractured relationship between the band members, especially his own estrangement from Waters. The album's title itself, The Division Bell, referenced the metaphorical divide within the band and, more broadly, the inability to communicate effectively both personally and within the context of the world at large.

"Keep Talking" and the Power of Speech

One of the album's most prominent tracks, "Keep Talking," was an anthem for communication in the face of division. The song's lyrics emphasized the importance of speaking, of breaking through barriers, and of refusing to allow silence and misunderstanding to persist. The track was a reflection of both the internal dynamics of Pink Floyd and broader social and political themes. It featured a famous sample of the voice of Stephen Hawking, who spoke about the nature of communication and the ability to transcend boundaries. The song's rich, atmospheric arrangement, with its synthesizers and Gilmour's soaring guitar solos, underscored the emotional weight of the lyrics, which were an open acknowledgment of the rift between Gilmour and Waters, as well as the band's fractured past.

"High Hopes" and Looking Toward the Future

"High Hopes," the final track on the album, is perhaps the most reflective of the themes of reconciliation and closure. In its contemplative lyrics and wistful melodies, the song expressed both regret and hope, acknowledging the band's past while simultaneously looking toward the future. Gilmour's lyrics here were some of his most personal, capturing a sense of bittersweet reflection on the journey of Pink Floyd and the relationships that had defined the band's music.

In The Division Bell, Pink Floyd confronted the divide between their creative past and present, offering a profound reflection on the consequences of miscommunication and the possibility of healing. It was an album that sought to find resolution without entirely erasing the difficulties of the past.

Pink Floyd's Legacy and the Band's Final Chapter

As The Division Bell was released in 1994, Pink Floyd's place in rock history was firmly secured. The band's legacy as pioneers of progressive rock and their contributions to the development of concept albums, innovative live performances, and sonic experimentation remained untouchable. However, with the completion of The Division Bell and the subsequent Division Bell Tour (1994), it became clear that Pink Floyd's time together as a unit was coming to an end.

The Final Tour and Growing Divisions

While the Division Bell Tour was a commercial and critical success, it also highlighted the internal struggles that still existed within the band. Despite the album's themes of communication and reconciliation, the personal rifts between Gilmour and Waters remained unresolved. Gilmour and Mason continued to carry the Pink Floyd torch, but their relationship with Waters was far from cordial. Waters, meanwhile, had embarked on his own successful solo career, which often reflected his own perspective on the band's breakup and the creative differences that had led to his departure.

Despite the growing tension, the Division Bell Tour was a testament to Pink Floyd's lasting power as a live act. The elaborate stage productions, the multimedia presentations, and the band's musicianship were as awe-inspiring as ever. The tour was a triumphant celebration of Pink Floyd's music, showcasing songs from The Wall, A Momentary Lapse of Reason, and The Division Bell to adoring audiences around the world.

However, by the end of the 1994 tour, it was clear that the band had reached the end of its natural life as a creative force. The members had come to terms with the fact that, without the unity that once defined them, Pink Floyd could not continue to evolve in the same way. Although they remained close collaborators and friends, the group officially dissolved after their final performances, with no further plans for future recordings or tours.

CHAPTER NINE

Beyond Pink Floyd: Solo Stardom

David Gilmour's transition from the frontman of Pink Floyd to a solo artist was a natural evolution in his musical career. While he had always been the defining guitarist and one of the primary creative forces behind Pink Floyd's sound, his solo work allowed him to explore new territory, showcase his personal musical vision, and experiment in ways that were not bound by the expectations of the band. On an Island (2006), Gilmour's third solo album, marked a significant milestone in his post-Pink Floyd career, receiving critical acclaim and further cementing his status as a respected solo artist. This chapter delves into the release of On an Island, its critical reception, Gilmour's evolution as a solo artist, and his collaborations, particularly with his wife Polly Samson. It also explores his live performances, culminating in the monumental Live at Pompeii (2017) project, which brought his solo work full circle and celebrated his legacy.

71

Release of On an Island (2006) and Critical Reception

After the conclusion of Pink Floyd's Division Bell Tour in 1994, Gilmour largely retreated from the public eye, focusing on family life and music outside the band context. However, the idea of releasing a new solo album had always been on his mind. His previous solo albums—David Gilmour (1978) and About Face (1984)—had been released in the wake of Pink Floyd's commercial successes, but they were relatively understated compared to the band's output. By 2006, however, Gilmour was ready to once again present his artistic vision to the world, and On an Island became his first major solo work in over 20 years.

The album was released in March 2006, and its arrival was eagerly anticipated by both longtime Pink Floyd fans and music critics alike. On an Island marked a departure from the more experimental soundscapes of Pink Floyd, instead embracing a more introspective, mellow, and atmospheric style. The album was a blend of classic rock influences and a more personal, reflective tone, showcasing Gilmour's mastery of melody and his ability to convey emotion through his guitar work. The title track, "On an Island," exemplified this with its hauntingly beautiful melody and meditative lyrics.

Critically, On an Island was widely praised for its warmth, depth, and emotional resonance. Reviewers noted the album's soft, understated quality—unlike the bombastic, conceptual works Gilmour had been involved with during his Pink Floyd years. It was an album about contemplation, personal reflection, and quiet beauty. The lush, dreamy atmospheres and Gilmour's signature guitar tone, combined with the lyrical contributions of Polly Samson, his wife and long-time collaborator, resonated deeply with listeners.

The album debuted at number one on the UK Albums Chart and reached the top 10 in several other countries, signaling a warm reception both commercially and critically. Gilmour's guitar work, as always, stood out—his tone was unmistakable, soulful, and filled with expressive bends and swells that conveyed profound emotion. The album featured guest contributions from a number of renowned musicians, including keyboardist Richard Wright (Gilmour's Pink Floyd bandmate), Roxy Music's Phil Manzanera, and Crosby, Stills & Nash. Their contributions helped shape the album's lush, atmospheric sound, giving it a depth that made it feel both intimate and expansive.

Gilmour's Evolution as a Solo Artist

David Gilmour's evolution as a solo artist is marked by his growing confidence and creative freedom, as he ventured into new musical territory without the constraints of Pink Floyd's established sound or the tension between band members. His solo work, while retaining elements of Pink Floyd's progressive rock foundation, has consistently emphasized introspection, lyricism, and an almost meditative quality that invites listeners to reflect.

Gilmour's solo albums are distinguished by his distinctive guitar playing—his famous emotive solos and ability to create atmosphere with just a few notes. While Pink Floyd's music had often been conceptual and grandiose, Gilmour's solo work allowed him to explore more personal themes, tackling matters like love, loss, and the passage of time in a more direct way. On an Island was a testament to this shift, with its relaxed pace and emotionally rich themes.

The lyrics, co-written with Polly Samson, reflect a sense of maturity and introspection. Many of the songs on On an Island deal with themes of nostalgia, solitude, and longing. Tracks like "The Blue" evoke deep emotional currents, exploring the natural world, human relationships, and the reflections that come with age. The collaboration between Gilmour and Samson became one of the defining aspects of his solo career, as her writing offered an emotional depth and lyrical complexity that resonated with Gilmour's musical style.

While his first solo albums had been more disjointed in their focus, On an Island marked a more coherent, focused work that brought Gilmour's songwriting and performance abilities into sharper view. It is clear that, free from the confines of Pink Floyd's expansive conceptual frameworks, Gilmour was able to find new avenues for creative exploration. This album established Gilmour not just as a talented guitarist, but as a skilled songwriter and vocalist in his own right.

Collaborations with Polly Samson

Polly Samson, Gilmour's wife and long-time collaborator, played a pivotal role in shaping the lyrical content of On an

Island and his later solo works. A novelist and lyricist in her own right, Samson's writing brought a level of emotional sophistication to Gilmour's music that enriched his sound and brought new depth to his solo projects.

Samson's contributions to On an Island helped elevate the album's themes of introspection and human connection. Her words captured the complexities of love, nature, and the passage of time, themes that complemented Gilmour's subtle, emotive musical arrangements. Their partnership, which blossomed in the 1990s, became one of the cornerstones of Gilmour's solo career, as the couple often co-wrote songs and worked together to craft an album that balanced musical beauty with profound emotional insight.

The creative synergy between Gilmour and Samson continued on his subsequent projects, including Rattle That Lock (2015), which further developed their artistic collaboration. Samson's influence on Gilmour's lyrics was undeniable, and her poetic, often mysterious style helped to solidify Gilmour's identity as a solo artist distinct from his Pink Floyd past.

Live Performances and Live at Pompeii (2017)

While Gilmour had always been an iconic live performer with Pink Floyd, his solo performances offered an entirely different experience. The more intimate setting of his solo concerts allowed him to explore his music in a deeply personal way, often adding new dimensions to his well-known Pink Floyd songs alongside his solo material.

After the release of On an Island, Gilmour embarked on a worldwide tour, performing the album live in concert, which included a performance at the Royal Albert Hall in London. The tour was a success, receiving positive reviews for Gilmour's masterful guitar playing and his ability to create a connection with the audience. His ability to hold an audience's attention with just his guitar, voice, and a handful of musicians was a testament to his strength as a solo performer, able to create an atmosphere of transcendence with even the most simple of notes.

Perhaps the crowning achievement of Gilmour's solo live career came with the release of Live at Pompeii in 2017. This project was a nod to the famous 1972 film Live at Pompeii, directed by Adrian Maben, which had captured Pink Floyd in their prime, performing live in the ancient Roman amphitheater. For Gilmour's Live at Pompeii, the project was not merely a nostalgic return to the past but a celebration of his evolution as an artist. Filmed during his 2016-2017 tour in support of Rattle That Lock, the performance was set against the stunning backdrop of the ancient Pompeii ruins.

The Live at Pompeii project was more than just a concert film—it was an exploration of Gilmour's solo music in the context of a legendary venue that had hosted some of rock's greatest live performances. The film combined his work from On an Island and Rattle That Lock with his Pink Floyd classics, creating a show that was intimate, epic, and emotionally resonant. It was an homage to Gilmour's roots in Pink Floyd while also showcasing his growth as a solo artist, able to command a space as a storyteller in his own right.

CHAPTER TEN

A Guitarist's Legacy

David Gilmour's influence on modern music, particularly in the realm of guitar playing, cannot be overstated. As one of the most iconic and respected guitarists of all time, his legacy transcends the confines of Pink Floyd and resonates throughout the entire rock genre. His unique blend of technical proficiency, emotive playing, and innovative sound design has inspired generations of musicians and guitarists. In this chapter, we will explore the depth of Gilmour's influence on the world of music, examining his signature techniques, the evolution of his gear, and the lasting impact of his iconic "Black Strat." Additionally, we will delve into his mentorship of young musicians and his continued support for the growth of the guitar community.

Gilmour's Influence on Modern Music and Guitar Playing

David Gilmour's approach to the guitar has left an indelible mark on modern music. While technically proficient, his style is defined not by speed or complexity but by its emotional depth and expressive power. His ability to convey emotion through his guitar—whether through subtle bends, soaring solos, or delicate phrasing—has made him one of the most influential guitarists in rock history.

Gilmour's legacy is not just about the sounds he created but also about the way he played. He was a master of restraint, knowing when to hold back and when to unleash the full force of his instrument. This ability to balance subtlety with intensity has influenced countless guitarists across multiple genres. His style is often described as "vocal" because of how closely it mimics the human voice, drawing listeners in with every note. The emotive quality of his solos, particularly in songs like "Comfortably Numb" and "Shine On You Crazy Diamond," is one of the reasons his playing has resonated so deeply with audiences worldwide.

Beyond his emotional expression, Gilmour's contributions to the development of guitar playing techniques have had a lasting effect on both seasoned professionals and aspiring musicians. His use of bending notes to create sustained, human-like vibrato is one of his signature techniques, and his ability to sustain notes with impeccable control has become one of his trademarks. Gilmour's precise use of the whammy bar to manipulate pitch and create textures, often in unexpected ways, has added to his allure as a guitarist who could create sounds that were both innovative and deeply moving.

Perhaps one of the most important aspects of Gilmour's influence is his use of tone. In an era when many guitarists were focused on speed and technicality, Gilmour emphasized tone above all else. His ability to craft a sound that was instantly recognizable—a balance of warmth, clarity, and sustain—has been a major influence on modern rock guitarists. From the experimental sounds on Meddle to the soaring leads on The Dark Side of the Moon, Gilmour's tone has shaped the sonic landscape of rock music, becoming a standard for aspiring guitarists to emulate.

His impact extends beyond the world of rock, as well. Gilmour's minimalist, yet emotionally powerful playing has inspired musicians across genres, including blues, jazz, and even classical music. Guitarists in all styles have drawn from his playing, finding inspiration in his ability to express complex emotions with just a few notes. From contemporary rock bands to experimental musicians, Gilmour's influence can be seen across many genres, where his mastery of tone and phrasing continues to inspire new generations of artists.

Signature Techniques, Gear, and the "Black Strat"

A key part of Gilmour's identity as a guitarist is his use of distinctive techniques and gear. His musical innovations were always closely tied to the instruments and tools he used, and his equipment choices have become as legendary as his playing. The most famous of these is his "Black Strat," a Fender Stratocaster that became synonymous with his sound.

The "Black Strat" has become one of the most iconic guitars in the history of rock. Purchased in 1970, this guitar was used on many of Pink Floyd's most famous recordings, including The

Dark Side of the Moon, Wish You Were Here, and The Wall. The guitar's simple yet elegant appearance—a black body with a white pickguard—belied its profound impact on rock music. Over the years, Gilmour customized the guitar with various modifications, including changes to the pickups and the bridge, which allowed him to fine-tune its sound to suit his needs. The "Black Strat" was responsible for much of the rich, creamy tone that defined Pink Floyd's sound, and its association with Gilmour made it one of the most instantly recognizable guitars in the world.

Gilmour's signature tone, however, was not only dependent on the "Black Strat" but also on the amplifiers and effects he used. His amp of choice for many years was a Hiwatt Custom 100, a powerful amplifier that allowed him to achieve a clean, uncolored sound with plenty of headroom. Gilmour was known for his minimalist approach to effects, often using a select few to enhance his tone. Key to his sound was the use of delay and reverb, which gave his solos their signature sense of space and depth. The Electro-Harmonix Holy Grail Reverb and the Electro-Harmonix Deluxe Memory Man delay pedal were staples of his rig, allowing him to create the atmospheric, expansive soundscapes for which he is famous.

A unique feature of Gilmour's playing was his skillful use of the guitar's tremolo arm, or whammy bar. Unlike many guitarists who use the whammy bar for extreme pitch bending, Gilmour employed it with a more subtle, nuanced approach. His use of the whammy bar to create swooping bends or gentle pitch variations added a layer of expressiveness to his solos, particularly on songs like "Shine On You Crazy Diamond" and "Comfortably Numb." This technique was part of Gilmour's overall philosophy that less is more—creating a signature sound without relying on excessive effects or technical flashiness.

Beyond the equipment, Gilmour's understanding of tone and sound engineering played a critical role in shaping his music. He often worked closely with engineers and producers to craft the perfect sound for each recording, whether it was for the precision-driven work of The Wall or the expansive sonic experiments of The Dark Side of the Moon. His knowledge of studio techniques and his innovative approach to sound manipulation contributed to the creation of Pink Floyd's rich, layered recordings.

Mentorship and Support for Upcoming Musicians

While Gilmour's music has influenced countless guitarists, he has also been a strong advocate for supporting younger musicians and helping them navigate the music industry. Throughout his career, Gilmour has worked with and mentored a number of up-and-coming guitarists, offering guidance and insight into both the technical and creative aspects of guitar playing.

Gilmour's willingness to collaborate with other musicians, whether through his solo work or in his role as a producer, has allowed him to pass on his knowledge and influence. He has been a champion of new talent, often featuring young musicians in his live performances or giving them opportunities to collaborate in the studio. For example, during the recording of On an Island, Gilmour worked with a range of musicians, including guitarist Chuck Leavell and keyboardist

Richard Wright, encouraging a collaborative spirit that fostered a supportive, creative environment.

In addition to his mentorship, Gilmour's own approach to guitar playing has been a source of inspiration for guitarists learning the craft. His emphasis on tone, feel, and expression over technical wizardry has led many to adopt a more soulful, nuanced approach to their instrument. Guitarists like Jonny Greenwood of Radiohead and David Bowie's guitarist Earl Slick have cited Gilmour as a major influence on their own playing, particularly in how they approach creating sound textures that evoke emotion. Gilmour's legacy as a mentor is seen in the way he has encouraged young musicians to embrace their individuality, focus on tone, and prioritize emotional expression over flashy virtuosity.

Additionally, Gilmour's support of various charitable initiatives and his involvement in causes such as Amnesty International and the Teenage Cancer Trust reflect his desire to give back to the music community. His charitable work has helped raise awareness and support for music education and the arts, ensuring that future generations of musicians have the opportunity to follow in his footsteps.

CHAPTER ELEVEN

Personal Life and Humanitarian Work

David Gilmour's life outside of music is just as fascinating as his legendary career with Pink Floyd. While many fans know him for his contributions to rock music, his private life and humanitarian efforts offer a more intimate look into the man behind the guitar. Throughout his life, Gilmour has maintained a relatively low profile, often shying away from the spotlight, preferring to let his music speak for him. However, when he does open up, whether about his personal life, his family, or his philanthropic endeavors, the world gets a glimpse of the values and principles that have guided him both as a musician and as a person. This chapter delves into Gilmour's family life, his long-lasting relationship with Polly Samson, his commitment to various charitable causes, and the insights into the man who helped shape the sound of an entire generation.

Family Life and Relationship with Polly Samson

David Gilmour's family life has been a cornerstone of his identity, offering him stability and grounding amid the pressures of fame. He has been married twice, with his most notable and lasting relationship being with writer and lyricist Polly Samson. Gilmour and Samson's relationship began in the early 1990s, and they have been together ever since, marrying in 1994. Their bond is not just personal but also professional, with Samson contributing lyrics to several of Gilmour's solo projects, including his 2006 album On an Island and his 2015 album Rattle That Lock.

The couple shares a deep connection, both romantically and creatively. Samson's literary sensibility has complemented Gilmour's music, adding a poetic depth to the lyrics of his later works. In fact, much of On an Island is imbued with a sense of intimacy and emotional depth that reflects their relationship. The album's lyrics, which deal with themes of love, loss, and reflection, draw heavily from the couple's shared experiences. Gilmour has described Samson as an integral part of his artistic process, with her ability to craft evocative, lyrical content providing a perfect balance to his music.

In addition to their musical partnership, Gilmour and Samson have four children together. Their family life has been relatively private, but it's clear that Gilmour values his role as a husband and father. His personal life stands in stark contrast to the tumultuous and often chaotic world of Pink Floyd, offering him a sense of calm and perspective. Gilmour has spoken on several occasions about how important his family is to him, often mentioning that his children have been a grounding influence in his life. Despite the demands of being a world-renowned musician, he has managed to strike a balance, creating a nurturing environment for his loved ones away from the public eye.

Gilmour has often praised Polly's influence on his life, calling her a source of strength and inspiration. She has also been a vocal supporter of his music and activism. Their partnership reflects a deep understanding of each other's creative process and a shared commitment to their values, both musically and personally.

Philanthropic Endeavors and Activism

While Gilmour is best known for his musical achievements, his humanitarian work and activism have played a significant role in his life. Throughout his career, Gilmour has been involved in various charitable efforts, using his fame and resources to support causes close to his heart. Much of his philanthropy has centered around human rights, environmental issues, and support for the arts.

One of Gilmour's primary philanthropic causes has been his commitment to environmental activism. He has been an outspoken advocate for climate change action, using his platform to raise awareness about the urgent need for global environmental reform. In the early 1990s, he became involved with organizations like Greenpeace, supporting their efforts to combat environmental degradation and preserve the planet's natural resources. Gilmour has also been a vocal critic of government policies that he believes are detrimental to the environment. He has taken part in numerous fundraising efforts, both through his music and public appearances, to raise funds for environmental initiatives.

Additionally, Gilmour has been deeply involved in supporting charities that focus on human rights, particularly those that promote freedom of expression, social justice, and the protection of vulnerable populations. He has performed at various benefit concerts, including the legendary Live 8 concert in 2005, which aimed to raise awareness about global poverty and the need for economic justice. Gilmour has also lent his voice to campaigns supporting the rights of refugees and immigrants, advocating for the fair treatment of those who have been displaced by war, poverty, and persecution.

Perhaps most notably, Gilmour has been a strong supporter of Amnesty International, an organization dedicated to protecting human rights worldwide. He has participated in multiple fundraising events for Amnesty and has spoken publicly about his admiration for the organization's work. His commitment to human rights is not just limited to his financial contributions but also to the causes he champions through his music. Songs like "Shine On You Crazy Diamond," "Mother," and "Another Brick in the Wall" have long been seen as critiques of social and political systems, adding a layer of activism to his art.

In addition to his work with environmental and human rights organizations, Gilmour has also been committed to supporting the arts. He has donated significant sums of money to various music charities, particularly those that help young musicians gain access to instruments and training. His personal donations and his participation in benefit concerts have allowed countless young artists to pursue their dreams, even in the face of financial adversity.

Insights into the Man Behind the Music

David Gilmour's public persona often stands in contrast to the tumultuous and high-drama world of rock 'n' roll. While Pink Floyd's history is filled with conflict, particularly between Gilmour and his former bandmate Roger Waters, Gilmour himself is known for his calm demeanor and stoic personality. He has never been one to court controversy or engage in the kind of public feuds that have often defined rock star culture. Instead, Gilmour has quietly forged his path, letting his music and personal values speak louder than any public statements.

A man of few words, Gilmour rarely gives interviews, and when he does, he is known for his modesty and humility. He often avoids discussing the more sensational aspects of his career, choosing instead to focus on the work itself. For Gilmour, the music has always come first. His focus on quality over quantity—whether in his guitar playing, his songwriting, or his approach to life—has defined his legacy. He is not a man of excess, nor is he driven by fame or wealth. His main priority has always been his family, his art, and his commitment to making the world a better place.

Despite his reserved nature, Gilmour has expressed a deep passion for the causes he supports. Whether discussing his commitment to environmental sustainability or his desire to see greater social justice in the world, Gilmour's sincerity is clear. His activism is driven not by the desire for recognition, but by a genuine concern for the well-being of others and the future of the planet.

Gilmour's humanity is evident in his music, which often reflects themes of introspection, empathy, and longing. His work with Pink Floyd, particularly on albums like The Dark Side of the Moon and The Wall, explored deep emotional landscapes, questioning the nature of human existence, mental health, and societal pressures. The vulnerability that Gilmour has conveyed through his guitar solos and lyrics has allowed listeners to connect with him on a deeply personal level.

As Gilmour approaches the later stages of his career, he remains an enigmatic figure—a man whose private life and humanitarian work stand as a testament to his values. His legacy will not only be defined by his music but by the integrity with which he has led his life. In an industry often characterized by excess and self-indulgence, David Gilmour has proven that it is possible to be both a rock star and a deeply grounded, compassionate individual. His story is one of balance, of blending the artistic with the ethical, and of using his talents for a greater good.

CHAPTER TWELVE

Awards and Recognition

David Gilmour's remarkable career as a guitarist, songwriter, and producer has earned him a wealth of accolades and recognition from both the music industry and fans worldwide. His contributions to Pink Floyd and his solo work have not only shaped the sound of progressive rock but have also inspired countless musicians and enthusiasts across generations. In this chapter, we explore the awards and honors Gilmour has received, both individually and as a member of Pink Floyd, and examine how these achievements reflect his profound impact on the music world.

Awards and Honors with Pink Floyd

As a core member of Pink Floyd, Gilmour played a pivotal role in creating some of the most iconic and critically acclaimed albums in music history. The band's innovative approach to sound and their ability to weave complex narratives through their music earned them widespread acclaim, translating into numerous prestigious awards.

Grammy Awards

Pink Floyd has been recognized multiple times by the Grammy Awards, winning their first in 1980 for The Wall (Best Engineered Album, Non-Classical). The album's theatrical soundscapes and the engineering work by James Guthrie, Roger Waters, and Gilmour himself were key to this achievement.

In 1995, the band won another Grammy for Marooned, an instrumental track from The Division Bell (Best Rock Instrumental Performance). Gilmour's atmospheric guitar work on the track is a prime example of his ability to evoke profound emotion through his instrument.

Several other nominations over the years, including for The Dark Side of the Moon and Wish You Were Here, solidified Pink Floyd's status as a Grammy favorite.

BRIT Awards

Pink Floyd won the BRIT Award for Outstanding Contribution to Music in 1995, recognizing their transformative influence on the British music scene and beyond. Gilmour accepted the award on behalf of the band, reflecting his central role in their legacy.

Rock and Roll Hall of Fame Induction

Pink Floyd received their induction into the Rock and Roll Hall of Fame in 1996. This honor acknowledged their innovative contributions to rock music and their status as one of the most successful and influential bands in history. During the induction, Gilmour was lauded for his unique guitar style and his role in shaping the band's distinctive sound.

UK Music Hall of Fame

Pink Floyd was admitted to the UK Music Hall of Fame in 2005. This recognition came on the heels of their reunion performance at the Live 8 concert, a historic moment that showcased the enduring power of their music.

Solo Recognition

While much of Gilmour's acclaim is tied to Pink Floyd, his solo career has also garnered significant recognition. His ability to craft deeply personal and resonant music outside the framework of the band has not gone unnoticed.

Ivor Novello Awards

Gilmour has been honored by the Ivor Novello Awards, which celebrate excellence in songwriting and composing. In 2008, he received the Lifetime Contribution to Music Award, a testament to his enduring influence as a composer and musician.

Q Awards

Gilmour won the Outstanding Contribution to Music Award at the Q Awards in 2008. This accolade highlighted his work both with Pink Floyd and as a solo artist, celebrating his dedication to musical innovation.

MOJO Awards

In 2006, Gilmour was presented with the MOJO Lifetime Achievement Award. This recognition coincided with the release of his critically acclaimed solo album On an Island, which demonstrated his ability to evolve as an artist while maintaining the essence of his iconic sound.

Grammy Nominations for Solo Work

Gilmour's solo projects have also been recognized by the Grammys. His 2006 live album Remember That Night, recorded at the Royal Albert Hall, earned nominations for its outstanding performances and production.

Impact on Guitar and Music Communities

David Gilmour's contributions to music have been celebrated not just through formal awards but also by the broader music and guitar communities. His innovative techniques, emotional playing style, and commitment to musical expression have earned him numerous accolades:

Rolling Stone's Greatest Guitarists

Gilmour consistently ranks among the greatest guitarists of all time in various publications, including Rolling Stone's definitive list. His unique ability to combine technical precision with raw emotion has solidified his reputation as one of the most influential guitarists in rock history.

Guitar Player Magazine

Gilmour has been awarded multiple Guitar Player Magazine Reader's Choice Awards for his unparalleled contributions to the instrument. His iconic solos, such as those in "Comfortably Numb" and "Shine On You Crazy Diamond," are often cited as some of the greatest in rock history.

Signature Gear and Tribute Models

The release of the Fender Custom Shop David Gilmour Signature Black Strat guitar in 2008 was a recognition of his influence on the guitar world. This model, designed in collaboration with Gilmour, pays homage to the instrument that shaped many of Pink Floyd's greatest songs.

Cultural and Lifetime Achievements

Beyond specific awards, Gilmour's legacy has been cemented through cultural honors and his status as a revered figure in the music world:

CBE Honor

In 2003, Gilmour was appointed a Commander of the Order of the British Empire (CBE) for his services to music. This prestigious honor reflected both his artistic contributions and his philanthropic efforts.

Honorary Doctorates

Gilmour has received honorary degrees from several institutions, including Anglia Ruskin University in his hometown of Cambridge. These honors celebrate his contributions to the arts and his impact on British culture.

Recognition at Live 8

While not a formal award, the emotional and critical response to Pink Floyd's reunion performance at Live 8 in 2005 was a powerful testament to Gilmour's enduring relevance. The performance, which marked the band's first reunion in decades, was hailed as one of the greatest live moments in rock history.

Fan and Peer Appreciation

While formal awards and honors are significant, the true measure of Gilmour's influence lies in the adoration of his fans and the respect of his peers. Fellow musicians have frequently cited him as a major influence, with artists across genres—from Eddie Van Halen to John Mayer—praising his tone, phrasing, and ability to convey deep emotion through his playing.

Fans, too, have been unwavering in their admiration. The enduring popularity of Pink Floyd and Gilmour's solo work, as well as the continued reverence for his guitar solos and live performances, highlight his lasting impact. Gilmour's humility and dedication to his craft have endeared him to millions worldwide.

Printed in Dunstable, United Kingdom

67663666R00060